Piggyback® Songs
For School

Compiled by
Jean Warren

Illustrated by Marion Hopping Ekberg
Chorded by Barbara Robinson

TOTLINE®
BOOKS

Warren Publishing House, Inc.
Everett, Washington

Dedication
For my Mother...who taught me
love...and then courage.

Marion Ekberg

Editorial Staff:

Gayle Bittinger, Kathleen Cubley, Brenda Warren, Jean Warren

Production Staff:

Manager: Eileen Carbary, *Assistant:* Jo Anna Brock

Book and Cover Design: Kathy Kotomaimoce

Computer Graphics: Carol DeBolt, Kathy Kotomaimoce, Eric Stovall

ISBN 0-911019-44-8

Library of Congress Catalog Number 85-50433
Printed in the United States of America
Published by: Warren Publishing House, Inc.
P.O. Box 2250
Everett, WA 98203

20 19 18 17 16 15 14 13 12 11 10 9 8 7 6 5

Contents

Starting the Year

First Day Of School

Sung to: *I'm a Little Teapot*

C   F   C
Good morning, Katie, how are you?
G₇   C G₇   C
This is the very first day of school.

I'm so glad to meet you,
F   C
Others will be too,
                 F
Just come in the classroom,
      C   G₇   C
There's lots of things to do.

Substitute the name of one of your children for the name *Katie.*

Kristina Carle and Nanette Belice
Kensington, MD

Brand New Year

Sung to: *London Bridge*

    C
It's time to start a brand new year,
G₇   C
Brand new year, brand new year.

It's time to start a brand new year,
G₇   C
Welcome new friends.

C
We'll learn lots of brand new things,
G₇   C
Brand new things, brand new things!

We'll learn lots of brand new things
G₇   C
Let's get started now.

Patricia Coyne
Mansfield, MA

Hello

Sung to: *Frere Jacques*

C
Hello, Shelley, hello, Shelley.

How are you? How are you?

We're so glad to have you,

We're so glad to have you.

Here at school, here at school.

Substitute the name of one of your children for the name *Shelley,* and the name of your group for the word *school.*

Linda Ferguson
Olympia, WA

Who Is Here Today?

Sung to: *Twinkle, Twinkle, Little Star*

C   F C
Let's see who is here today,
G₇   C G₇   C
Who has come to join our play?
    G₇   C   G₇
Everyone sit close at hand,
C   G₇   C   G₇
Say your name, then you can stand.
C   F C
Let's see who is here today,
G₇   C   G₇   C
Who has come to join our play?

Ellen Bedford
Bridgeport, CT

Hello Song
Sung to: *Three Blind Mice*

C   G₇ C   G₇ C
Hello, Jamie. Hello, Jamie.

     G₇ C   G₇ C
How are you? How are you?

             G₇   C
We're glad you're here to laugh and play,

         G₇   C
We hope you'll have some fun today,

        G₇   C
You're welcome, welcome everyday.

  G₇   C
To our playschool.

Substitute the name of one of your children for the name *Jamie*, and the name of your group for the word *playschool*.

Bev Qualheim
Marquette, MI

Glad to See You
Sung to: *Frere Jacques*

Teacher:
C
I'm Ms. Baker, I'm Ms. Baker.

That's my name, that's my name.

Glad to see you here,

Glad to see you here.

What's your name? What's your name?

Child:
C
I am Bobby, I am Bobby.

That's my name, that's my name.

I am glad to be here,

I am glad to be here.

At school today, at school today.

Substitute your name and the name of one of your children for the names *Ms. Baker* and *Bobby*.

Betty Ruth Baker
Waco, TX

Have You Met a Friend Of Mine?

Sung to: *The Muffin Man*

F
Have you met a friend of mine,
  G₇   C
A friend of mine, a friend of mine?
F
Have you met a friend of mine?
G C   F
Her name is Joanie.

Substitute one of your children's names for the
name *Joanie.*

Julie Israel
Ypsilanti, MI

What Is Your Name?

Sung to: *Frere Jacques*

C
What is your name? What is your name?

Tell us please, tell us please.

We would like to meet you,

We would like to meet you.

What's your name? What's your name?

Betty Silkunas
Lansdale, PA

Where, Oh Where?

Sung to: *Paw, Paw Patch*

F
Where, oh where, oh where is Ryan?

C₇
Where, oh where, oh where is Ryan?

F
Where, oh where, oh where is Ryan?

   C₇   F
He's waving his hand for all to see.

   F
He's slowly walking around the circle,

   (Children clap hands.)

   C₇
He's slowly walking around the circle.

   F
He's slowly walking around the circle,

   C₇   F
He's waving his hand for all to see.

Substitute the name of one of your children for the name *Ryan*. Substitute other actions such as *hopping, crawling* or *tiptoeing* for *walking*.

Susan Miller
Kutztown, PA

Let's Clap And Jump

Sung to: *The Farmer In the Dell*

       D
We're happy Hope is here,

We're happy Hope is here.

Let's clap and jump and turn around,

          A₇   D
We're happy Hope is here.

Substitute the name of one of your children for the name *Hope*. Have that child stand in the center of the circle or next to you as the song is sung. Then let that child choose the next child to be sung to.

Rita Galloway
Harlingen, TX

Who Are You?

Sung to: *Twinkle, Twinkle, Little Star*

C   F   C
I am Betsy, who are you?

(Points to another child.)

G₇   C   G₇   C
I am Kenny, how about you?

(Chooses new child.)

    G₇   C   G₇
I am Annie, who are you?

(Points to another child.)

C   G₇   C   G₇
I am Jason, how about you?

(Chooses new child.)

C   F   C
I am Kathy, who are you?

(Points to another child.)

G₇   C G₇   C
I am Peter, how about you?

Substitute the names of your children for the names in the song. Repeat the song until each child has had a chance to introduce him or herself.

Bev Qualheim
Marquette, MI

Hello, New Friend

Sung to: *Frere Jacques*

C
My name is Ben, my name is Ben.

(Child points to self as the group sings his name.)

What is yours? What is yours?

(Child points to another child, that child says his or her name.)

How are you today, Sue?

Very well, I thank you.

Hello, new friend; hello, new friend.

Substitute the names of your children for the names *Ben* and *Sue*.

Susan Miller
Kutztown, PA

Shake Your Hand
Sung to: *Old MacDonald Had a Farm*

F   B♭   F
He would like to shake your hand,

           C₇   F
And say hello to you.

           B♭   F
He will tell you his name's Kelly,

      C₇   F
Now tell him your name too.

(Child says name.)

Hello, Susie; hello, Susie; hello, hello, hello, Susie.

           B♭   F
He would like to shake your hand,

(Shake hands.)

      C₇ F
And say hello to you.

Substitute the names of your children for the names *Kelly* and *Susie*. Continue singing the song until each child has had a chance to shake someone's hand.

Patricia Coyne
Mansfield, MA

The Name Game
Sung to: *The Muffin Man*

F
Welcome, welcome, all my friends.

      G₇   C₇
We'll learn your names through this game.

F
Stand up, Nick, it is your turn

G₇   C₇   F
Take a block and then return.

Place one block for each child in a pile. Have the children sit in a circle around the blocks. Sing a verse for one of your children. Have the child named stand up, take one of the blocks and return to his or her place. Repeat until each child has had a turn.

Susan M. Paprocki
Northbrook, IL

Time For School

We Like to Come to School

Sung to: *The Farmer In the Dell*

D
We like to come to school,

We like to come to school.

Our school is such a happy place,

    A₇   D
We like to come to school.

Substitute the words *terrific, great, yummy, friendly, fun, exciting,* etc., for the word *happy.* Or ask the children for suggestions.

Ann-Marie Donovan
Framingham, MA

It's Time to Go to School

Sung to: *She'll Be Coming Round the Mountain*

F
It is time to go to school, here we come,

                          C₇
It is time to go to school, here we come.

F
It is time to go to school,

      B♭
We think school is pretty cool,

F   C₇   F
It is time to go to school, here we come.

Judy Hall
Wytheville, VA

I Like to Go to School

Sung to: *The Farmer In the Dell*

D
I like to go to school,

I like to go to school.

Heigh-ho-the-derry-oh,

A₇   D
I like to go to school.

Additional verses: I like to look at books; I like to build with blocks; I like to listen to stories; I like to draw and paint; I like to sing new songs; I like to play with friends.

Betty Ruth Baker
Waco, TX

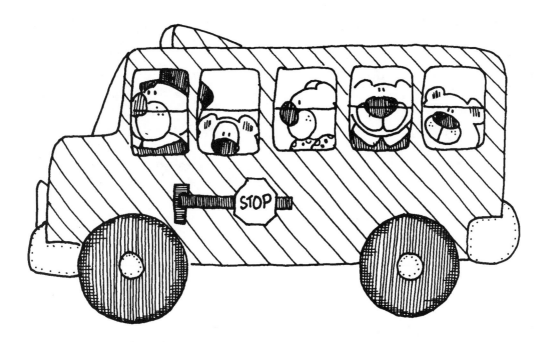

Off to School We Go

Sung to: *A-Hunting We Will Go*

C
Off to school we go,

  G
It's off to school we go.

  C   F
We'll take our lunch and ride the bus,

  C G   C
With everyone we know.

C
Off to school we go,

  G
It's off to school we go.

  C   F
We learn our ABC's and more,

   C G   C
With everyone we know.

Judy Hall
Wytheville, VA

Waiting For the Bus

Sung to: *Frere Jacques*

C
I am waiting, I am waiting,

For the bus, for the bus.

When will it get here?

Hopefully it is near.

Here it comes, here it comes.

Lindsay Hall
Wytheville, VA

Down At the Bus Stop
Sung to: *Down By the Station*

C
Down at the bus stop
G   C
Early in the morning,

See all the children,
G   C
Everyone we know.

Waiting for the school bus
G   C
Safely on the sidewalk,

Honk-honk, beep-beep,
G   C
Off we go.

Judy Hall
Wytheville, VA

The Children On the Bus
Sung to: *The Wheels On the Bus*

          F
The children on the bus sit nice and quiet,
C   F
Nice and quiet, nice and quiet.

The children on the bus sit nice and quiet
C   F
When we take a ride.

          F
The children on the bus look out the window,
C   F
Out the window, out the window.

The children on the bus look out the window
C   F
When we take a ride.

          F
The children on the bus stay in their seats,
C   F
In their seats, in their seats.

The children on the bus stay in their seats
C   F
When we take a ride.

Create additional verses as desired.

Cindy Dingwall
Palatine, IL

To Our School

Sung to: *Over the River And Through the Woods*

C
Over the bridges and through the streets
   F   G₇   C
It's to our school we go.
   F   C
The drivers know the way to go
     G₇   C
As they drive us safe and slow.

C
Over the bridges and through the streets
   F   G₇   C
In rain and sleet and snow.
     F   C
They drive with care, they get us there
   G₇   C
As over the streets we go.

Judy Hall
Wytheville, VA

Early Morning Schoolyard

Sung to: *Down By the Station*

C
Down by the schoolyard
G   C
Early in the morning,

See the yellow buses
G   C
Lining up so well.

Dropping off the children
G   C
Going to their classrooms,

Bong-bong, ding-dong,
G   C
There's the bell.

Judy Hall
Wytheville, VA

We Welcome You

Sung to: *Mary Had a Little Lamb*

C
We welcome you to school today,
G₇   C
School today, school today.

We welcome you to school today,
G₇   C
Please come in and play.

C
We're glad to have you here today,
G₇   C
Here today, here today.

We're glad to have you here today.
   G₇   C
Yes, it's a special day!

Deborah A. Roessel
Flemington, NJ

Welcome to Our School

Sung to: *The Paw Paw Patch*

F
Brian, welcome to our school,
C₇
Brian, welcome to our school,
F
Brian, welcome to our school,
    C₇   F
We're so glad that you are here with us.

Substitute the name of one of your children for the
name *Brian,* and the name of your group for the word
school.

Ann-Marie Donovan
Framingham, MA

I Want to Say Hello

Sung to: *I'm a Little Teapot*

C   F C
I am your new teacher, Mrs. Coyne,
G₇   C G₇ C
I want to say hello to you.
C   F   C
We will learn our letters and numbers too,
      G₇   C
We'll have fun and learn lots too!

Substitute your name for the name *Mrs. Coyne.*

Patricia Coyne
Mansfield, MA

I'm So Glad You Came

Sung to: *London Bridge*

C
Welcome to school today,
G   C
School today, school today.

Welcome to school today,
G   C
I'm so glad you came.

C
My name is Mrs. Brown,
G   C
Mrs. Brown, Mrs. Brown.

My name is Mrs. Brown,
G   C
I'm so glad you came.

Substitute your name for the name *Mrs. Brown.*

Karen Brown
Siloam Springs, AR

Welcome to Our Class

Sung to: *Little White Duck*

C   F
It's time to meet Adam,
                C₇
Who's come to our class.

It's time to meet Adam,
               F
Who's starting school today.
   B♭   F
We know that we'll have so much fun,
       G₇   C₇
That we'll say to ourselves when the day is done,
F   C₇
Hurray, Adam came to be in our class.
   C   C₇   F
Hurray, hurray, hurray.

Substitute the name of your new student or the name
of a visitor for the name *Adam.*

Ellen Javernick
Loveland, CO

Welcome Song

Sung to: *Oh, My Darling Clementine*

   F
Little Reid, little Reid,
           C₇
Little Reid is new today,
                        F
We are glad you've joined our classroom,
     C₇   F
And we hope that you will stay.

Substitute the name of your new student for the name
Reid, and the name of your group for the word
classroom.

Judy Hall
Wytheville, VA

We're So Glad

Sung to: *If You're Happy And You Know It*

      G   D
We're so glad you've come to school today,

                                   G
We're so glad you've come to school today.

C
Kristy won't you stand,

    G
And shake Linda's hand.

    D   G
Now everybody clap and say ole'!

      G   D
We're so glad you've come to school today,

                                   G
We're so glad you've come to school today.

C
Elizabeth stamp your feet,

    G
And Eric smile so sweet.

    D   G
Now everybody clap and say ole'.

      G   D
We're so glad you've come to school today,

                                   G
We're so glad you've come to school today.

C
Susan take a bow,

    G
And Kevin blink right now.

    D   G
Now everybody stand and say ole'!

      G   D
We're so glad you've come to school today,

                                   G
We're so glad you've come to school today.

C
Eileen hop about,

    G
And David give a shout.

    D   G
Now everybody clap and say ole'!

      G   D
We're so glad you've come to school today,

                                   G
We're so glad you've come to school today.

C
Kathleen touch your chin,

    G
And Dorothy show a grin.

    D   G
Now everybody clap and say ole'!

Substitute the names of your children for the names in the song. Have the children act out the motions as their names are called.

Marie Wheeler
Tacoma, WA

I'm Glad You Came to School

Sung to: *The Farmer In the Dell*

D
I'm glad you came to school,

I'm glad you came to school.

I've planned lots of fun for you,
      A₇   D
I'm glad you came to school.

D
It's time for you to go,

It's time for you to go.

I'll see you tomorrow,
      A₇   D
But now it's time to go.

Sue Brown
Louisville, KY

Welcome

Sung to: *Happy Birthday*

  F   C
We welcome you here,
         F
We welcome you here.
         B♭
We welcome everybody,
  F   C F
We welcome you here.

Judy Hall
Wytheville, VA

Happy Faces

Sung to: *Jingle Bells*

F
Smiling faces, happy faces,

Giggling all around.
C₇   F
Oh, what fun we'll have this way
G₇   C₇
In a happy class today.
F
He-he-he, he-he-he,

He-he-he-he-he.
C₇   F
Ha-ha-ha, ha-ha-ha-ha,
     C₇   F
In a happy class today!

Susan Peters
Upland, CA

Starting the Day
Sung to: *Mary Had a Little Lamb*

C
Merrily we start the day,
G   C
Start the day, start the day.

Merrily we start the day,
G   C
All of us at school.

Judy Hall
Wytheville, VA

School's Begun
Sung to: *Twinkle, Twinkle, Little Star*

C   F   C
Ding-dong, ding-dong, school's begun,
G₇   C   G₇   C
Ding-dong, ding-dong, let's have fun.
C   F   C
Learning our numbers, colors too,
G₇   C   G₇   C
And our letters just for you.
C   F   C
Ding-dong, ding-dong, school's begun,
G₇   C   G₇   C
Ding-dong, ding-dong, let's have fun.

Judy Hall
Wytheville, VA

Let's Work And Play
Sung to: *Sailing, Sailing*

C
Welcome, children,
         F   C
We're glad you're here today.
       G₇   C
We're going to work, we're going to play,
D   G₇
All along the way.
C
Welcome, children,
F   C
Stay with us a while.
    G₇   C
I'm sure you'll have a special day
       D   G   C
And leave here with a smile.

Judy Hall
Wytheville, VA

Morning Greeting
Sung to: *Down By the Station*

G   D₇   G
Outside the schoolroom early in the morning,
                D₇   G
See the happy children standing straight and tall.

Now we see the teacher,
D₇   G
Greet the waiting children,
     D₇   G
Come in children one and all.

Ellen Javernick
Loveland, CO

Greeting Song

Sung to: *The Farmer In the Dell*

Teacher:

D
I'm glad you came today,

I'm glad you came today.

Hello, hello to everyone,

(Wave hello.)

A₇   D
I'm glad you came today.

Children:

D
We're glad we came today,

We're glad we came today.

Hello, hello to everyone,

(Wave hello.)

A₇   D
We're glad we came today.

All:

D
We'll work and play today,

We'll work and play today.

Hello, hello to everyone,

(Wave hello.)

A₇   D
We'll work and play today.

Betty Ruth Baker
Waco, TX

Start the Day With a Smile

Sung to: *The Mulberry Bush*

C
This is the way we start the day,

G
Start the day, start the day.

C
This is the way we start the day,

G   C
So early in the morning.

C
First we smile and shake a hand,

G
Shake a hand, shake a hand.

C
First we smile and shake a hand,

G   C
So early in the morning.

C
Then we sit down quietly,

G
Quietly, quietly.

C
Then we sit down quietly,

G   C
So early in the morning.

C
We listen very carefully,

G
Carefully, carefully.

C
We listen very carefully,

G   C
So early in the morning.

Rita Galloway
Harlingen, TX

Hello, Children

Sung to: *Goodnight Ladies*

C   G₇
Hello, children; hello, children,
C F   C   G₇ C
Hello, children; I'm glad you're here today.

Judy Hall
Wytheville, VA

Exciting Day

Sung to: *Row, Row, Row Your Boat*

 C
It's time, time, time to start,

Time to start the day.

We will finish all our work,
 G   C
And then we'll stop and play.

Kristina Carle and Nanette Belice
Kensington, MD

A Happy Start

Sung to: *Skip to My Lou*

    F
Let's start the day in a happy way,
    C₇
Let's start the day in a happy way,
    F
Let's start the day in a happy way,
C₇   F
Let's get ready to learn and play.

Tami Hall
Owasso, OK

How Are You This Morning?

Sung to: *Frere Jacques*

C
Good morning, good morning,

How are you? How are you?

It sure is good to see you,

It sure is good to see you.

We'll have fun, we'll have fun.

Cindy Dingwall
Palatine, IL

Join Us In the Circle

Sung to: *Yankee Doodle*

C   G₇
Join us in the circle, please,
C   G₇
Find a special place.
C
Cross your legs,
    F
No wiggles, please,
G₇   C
Show us your smiling face.
F
Join us in the circle, please,
C
Find a special place.
F
Cross your legs,

No wiggles, please,
      C   G₇   C
Show us your smiling face.

Betty Silkunas
Lansdale, PA

I'm Ready

Sung to: *I'm a Little Teapot*

C *in Rm 14*   F   C
I'm a little helper, look at me,
G₇   C   G₇   C
I'm as busy as I can be.
I'm nice to everyone
       my things F   C
I put away the toys as you can see,
          F   G₇   C
I'm ready for the circle, look at me.
        learning

Betty Ruth Baker
Waco, TX

Wiggles

Sung to: *I'm a Little Teapot*

C
Wiggles in my pockets
F   C
Get them out,
G₇   C
Wiggles in my socks
    G₇   C
I wiggle them out

                    F   C
Wiggles and waggles and woggles and shouts,
         F   G₇   C
I'll waggle and woggle those wiggles right out!

Michele Triplett
Peoria, IL

Circle Time

Sung to: *London Bridge*

C
See the circles on the floor,
G   C
On the floor, on the floor.

See the circles on the floor,
G   C
On the floor.

C
Find a circle and stand on one,
G   C
Stand on one, stand on one.

Find a circle and stand on one,
G   C
Stand on one.

C
Fold your legs and sit right down,
G   C
Sit right down, sit right down.

Fold your legs and sit right down,
G   C
Sit right down.

C
Let's all listen to the teacher,
G   C
To the teacher, to the teacher.

Let's all listen to the teacher,
G   C
It is circle time.

Make circles on the floor in any arrangement using construction paper, masking tape, etc. As you sing the song, have the children follow the directions.

Lois Olson
Webster City, IA

Are You Ready?

Sung to: *Frere Jacques*

C
Are you ready? Are you ready?

   (Clap.)

Please sit down, please sit down.

   (Sit down.)

Time to quiet down now, time to quiet down now,

   (Put finger on lips.)

Hands on laps, hands on laps.

   (Place hands on lap.)

Ellen Javernick
Loveland, CO

Special Things
Sung to: *Jingle Bells*

F
Show and tell, show and tell,

Show and tell today.
C₇   F
Come and share your special things
    G₇   C₇
You brought along the way.
F
Show and tell, show and tell,

Show and tell today.
C₇   F
Come and share your special things
    C₇   F
You brought with you today.

Judy Hall
Wytheville, VA

It's Time For Show And Tell
Sung to: *The Farmer In the Dell*

          D
It's time for show and tell,

It's time for show and tell.

Hey, hey, it's lots of fun,
              A₇   D
It's time for show and tell.

Cindy Dingwall
Palatine, IL

Sharing Time
Sung to: *Twinkle, Twinkle, Little Star*

C   F   C
Won't you share your show and tell?
G₇   C   G₇   C
We will look and listen well.

            G₇   C   G₇
We know our turn will come soon
C   G₇   C   G₇
So we sing this little tune.
C   F   C
Won't you share your show and tell?
G₇   C   G₇   C
We will look and listen well.

Betty Silkunas
Lansdale, PA

Lots to See

Sung to: *I'm a Little Teapot*

C
Show and tell is great,
    F   C
There's lots to see.
  G₇   C
It's fun for you,
     G₇   C
And it's fun for me.
                F C
Showing things to others is a joy,
      G₇   C
For every little girl and boy.

Susan Burbridge
Beavercreek, OH

Show And Tell

Sung to: *Mary Had a Little Lamb*

C
It's Joey's turn for show and tell,
G₇   C
Show and tell, show and tell.

It's Joey's turn for show and tell,
G₇   C
Let's see what he brought.

Substitute the name of one of your children for the name *Joey*.

Ann-Marie Donovan
Framingham, MA

Let Us See It

Sung to: *London Bridge*

C
Eddie brought his show and tell,
G   C
Show and tell, show and tell.

Eddie brought his show and tell,
G   C
With him today.

C
Take it out and show us now,
G   C
Show us now, show us now.

Take it out and show us now,
G   C
Let us see it.

Substitute the name of one of your children for the name *Eddie*.

Judy Hall
Wytheville, VA

Ready to Share

Sung to: *If You're Happy And You Know It*

              G   D
If you're ready to share, clap your hands,
                         G
If you're ready to share, slap your knees.
          C
If you're ready to share,
        G
Then quiet you will be.
        D   G
If you're ready to share, fold your hands.

Susan Peters
Upland, CA

Sharing
Sung to: *The Farmer In the Dell*

D
It's Jeff's turn to share,

It's Jeff's turn to share.

Let's look and see what Jeff has brought

A₇   D
It's Jeff's turn to share.

Susbstitute the name of one of your children for the name *Jeff*.

Paula Laughtland
Edmonds, WA

I'm a Little Excited
Sung to: *I'm a Little Teapot*

C   F   C
I'm a little excited, ready to start,

G₇   C   G₇   C
Here is my toy, I'm in my spot.

                          F   C
When I get a turn I'll tell all about,

                          G₇   C
How special my toy is inside and out.

Susan Peters
Upland, CA

What's Inside?
Sung to: *Mary Had a Little Lamb*

C
Amy has a mystery bag,

G₇   C
Mystery bag, mystery bag.

Amy has a mystery bag,

  G₇   C
I wonder what's inside.

C
She will give us all a clue,

G₇   C
All a clue, all a clue.

She will give us all a clue,

  G₇   C
To help guess what's inside.

C
We will have to make a guess,

G₇   C
Make a guess, make a guess.

We will have to make a guess,

  G₇   C
To find out what's inside.

This is a group problem-solving activity. Have the children bring their show and tell items in bags. After you sing this song for one of your children, have that child give clues about what's in his or her bag while the other children try to guess what it is.

Ann-Marie Donovan
Framingham, MA

Time For Stories
Sung to: *Oh, My Darling Clementine*

C
Time for stories, time for stories,
G₇
Time for stories today,
C
Let's sit down, let's be quiet,
G₇   C
Wonder what we'll hear today?

Cindy Dingwall
Palatine, IL

I'm a Ready Listener
Sung to: *I'm a Little Teapot*

C   F   C
I'm a ready listener, read me a book,
G₇   C   G₇   C
Hands in my lap, at the teacher I look.
F   C
When I get all ready the teacher will say,
F   G₇   C
"This is the story that I have for you today."

Tami Hall
Owasso, OK

If You're Ready
Sung to: *If You're Happy And You Know It*

G   D
If you're ready for a story, find a seat,
G
If you're ready for a story, find a seat.
C
If you're ready for a story,
G
Check your hands and then your feet.
D   G
If you're ready for a story, find a seat.

Sue Brown
Louisville, KY

Guess What It's Time to Do

Sung to: *Oh, Dear, What Can the Matter Be?*

C
Oh, my, guess what it's time to do,
G₇
Oh, my, guess what it's time to do,
C
Oh, my, guess what it's time to do,
G₇   C
Come over here and find out.

Cindy Dingwall
Palatine, IL

Be As Quiet As Can Be

Sung to: *Oh, My Darling Clementine*

                F
Let's sit down, let's sit down,
                        C₇
Let's sit down so quietly,
                                F
Let's sit down, let's sit down,
        C₇   F
Be as quiet as can be!

Additional verses: Let's stand up; Let's line up.

Lois Putnam
Pilot Mt., NC

Transition Time

Sung to: *Mary Had a Little Lamb*

C
All the people wearing green,
G   C
Wearing green, wearing green.

All the people wearing green,
        G₇   C
Stand by the door right now.

Substitute such characteristics as *born in June; with brown hair*, etc., for *wearing green*; and the appropriate action for *stand by the door.*

Ellen Javernick
Loveland, CO

If Your Name Begins With A

Sung to: *If You're Happy And You Know It*

                G   D
If your name begins with A, wash your hands,

                                        G
If your name begins with A, wash your hands.
        C
If your name begins with A,
        G
If your name begins with A,
        D   G
If your name begins with A, wash your hands.

Susbstitute other letters for the letter A and names of other activities for *wash your hands.*

Betty Silkunas
Lansdale, PA

Away We Go
Sung to: *The Farmer In the Dell*

D
Playtime is here,

Playtime is here.

Heigh-ho and away we go,
    A₇   D
Playtime is here.

Substitute other special times such as *snacktime, lunchtime, naptime,* etc., for *playtime.*

Jean Warren

Please Be Quiet
Sung to: *Oh, My Darling Clementine*

        F
Please be quiet, please be quiet,
        C₇
Please be quiet just now.
       F
Sh-sh-sh-sh, sh-sh-sh-sh,

   (Put finger to lips.)

     C₇   F
Please be quiet just now.

Lois Putnam
Pilot Mt., NC

It's Time
Sung to: *The Farmer In the Dell*

D
It's time to come to group,

It's time to come to group.

Come on over, find a seat,
    A₇   D
It's time to come to group.

Sue Brown
Louisville, KY

Snack Attack

Sung to: *Three Blind Mice*

C   G₇ C   G₇ C
Snack attack, snack attack,

          G₇   C   G₇   C
A snack for us to eat, let's sit in our seats.

       G₇   C
Peanuts or raisins or cheese would be great,

     G₇   C
Even bananas, I just can't wait,

     G₇   C
Hurry now, let's not be late.

     G₇ C
Snack attack.

Carol Kyger
Hood River, OR

Snack Time

Sung to: *I'm a Little Teapot*

C   F   C
It is time for us to have our snack,

G₇   C   G₇   C
Please sit down and hands in your lap.

               F   C
Wait 'til everyone is served their food,

         F   G₇   C
Then eat your snack; yum, yum, it's good.

Patricia Coyne
Mansfield, PA

Get Ready For Snacks

Sung to: *Up On the Housetop*

F
Let's get ready for snacks today,

B♭   F   C
See the clock, what does it say?

F
Time to put the toys away.

B♭   F   C   F
Hear your teacher, what does (he/she) say?

B♭   F
Wash your hands 'til they are clean,

C   F
All around and in between.

         F₇   B♭ F B♭
Walk back quietly to your seats,

F   C   C₇   F
Now you're ready for your good treats.

Florence Dieckmann
Roanoke, VA

We Love It So

Sung to: *The Farmer In the Dell*

D
It's time to have a snack,

It's time to have a snack.

Yum, yum, we love it so,
A₇   D
It's time to have a snack.

D
We'll have to wash our hands,

We'll have to wash our hands.

Yum, yum, we love it so,
A₇   D
We'll wash before we snack.

D
We'll eat a healthful treat,

We'll eat a healthful treat.

Yum, yum, we love it so,
A₇   D
We'll eat a healthful treat.

Cindy Dingwall
Palatine, IL

Now It's Time For Snack

Sung to: *Here We Go Looby Loo*

C
Now it is time for snack,
          G₇
Now it is time for snack,
C
Now it is time for snack,
    G₇   C
We will sit down and eat crackers.

Substitute the name of the day's snack for the word *crackers*.

Susan Miller
Kutztown, PA

Lunch With All the Bunch

Sung to: *The Muffin Man*

F
Now it's time to have some lunch,
G₇   C₇
Time to lunch with all the bunch.
F
Now it's time to have some lunch,
    G₇   C₇   F
Let's munch with all the bunch.

Betty Silkunas
Lansdale, PA

It's Off to Lunch We Go

Sung to: *A-Hunting We Will Go*

      F
It's off to lunch we go,

It's off to lunch we go.

The food tastes very yummy,
                 C   F
And helps us all to grow.

Judy Hall
Wytheville, VA

I'm Getting Very Hungry

Sung to: *Frere Jacques*

C
Time for lunch, time for lunch,

Let's get ready, let's get ready.

I'm getting very hungry,

I'm getting very hungry.

How 'bout you? How 'bout you?

C
Wash our hands, wash our hands,

Before we eat, before we eat.

We should have clean hands,

We should have clean hands.

When we eat, when we eat.

C
Let's sit down, let's sit down,

Quietly, quietly.

Wait 'til we are served,

Wait 'til we are served.

Before we eat, before we eat.

C
Use table manners, use table manners,

Let's be polite, let's be polite.

Remember please and thank you,

Remember please and thank you,

When we eat, when we eat.

Cindy Dingwall
Palatine, IL

Lunchtime

Sung to: *Alouette*

F
It's time for lunch now,
C₇   F
Yes, it's time for lunch now.

It's time for lunch now,
C₇   F
Everyone line up.

Think of all the food we'll eat,

Think of all the food we'll eat.
C
Sandwiches, vegetables,

Milk and meat.
F
It's time for lunch now,
C₇   F
Yes, it's time for lunch now.

It's time for lunch now,
C₇   F
Everyone line up.

Judy Hall
Wytheville, VA

Wash For Lunch

Sung to: *London Bridge*

C
We have washed our hands and faces,
G   C
Hands and faces, hands and faces.

We have washed our hands and faces,
G   C
May we eat lunch now?

Additional verses: Germs are gone, they've left no traces; We are sitting in our places.

Becky Valenick
Rockford, IL

Lunchtime Rap

Sung to: *Teddy Bear, Teddy Bear*

F
Children, children, it's time to eat,
C₇
Go wash your hands and have a seat.
F
Serve the food and eat it up,
                        C   F
Talk with your friends and then clean up.

Nanette Belice and Kristina Carle
Kensington, MD

Close Your Eyes

Sung to: *Rock-A-Bye, Baby*

C   G₇
Now it is time for us to rest,

       C
Close your eyes and do your best.

       G₇
I'll stay with you while you sleep,

C   F G₇ C
When you awake, we'll do something neat.

Cindy Dingwall
Palatine, IL

Time to Rest

Sung to: *Oh, My Darling Clementine*

C
Time to rest, time to rest,

      G₇
Sleepy heads, it's time rest.

        C
When you wake up you'll feel so good,

   G₇
That you'll do your very best!

Janice Bodenstedt
Jackson, MI

It Is Naptime

Sung to: *Frere Jacques*

C
It is naptime, it is naptime,

Come along, come along.

Go and get your mat now,

Time to take a nap now.

Let's all rest, let's all rest.

Judy Hall
Wytheville, VA

Jump And Hop

Sung to: *In And Out the Window*

      F   C
Jump up and down just like this,

                         F
Jump up and down just like this,

                         C
Jump up and down just like this,

                    F
Jump and jump and jump.

Additional verses: Hop up and down just like this; Stretch up and down just like this; Bounce up and down just like this; Pop up and down just like this; etc.

Lois Putnam
Pilot Mt., NC

Hop, Hop All Around

Sung to: *Skip to My Lou*

F
Hop, hop, all around,
C₇
Hop, hop, on the ground.
F
Hop, hop, don't you stop,
C₇   F
Hop until you drop, drop, drop.

Additional verses: March, march all around; Jump, jump all around; Crawl, crawl all around.

Lois Putnam
Pilot Mt., NC

Put Your Hands Up to the Sky

Sung to: *Mary Had a Little Lamb*

C
Put your hands up to the sky,
G₇   C
To the sky, to the sky.

Put your hands up to the sky,
         G₇   C
And see if you can fly.

C
Put your hands down on the floor,
G₇   C
On the floor, on the floor.

Put your hands down on the floor,
    G₇   C
And try to count to four.

C
Now put both hands in your lap,
G₇   C
In your lap, in your lap.

Now put both hands in your lap,
    G₇   C
And take a little nap.

Have the children act out the motions as you sing the song.

Linda Ferguson
Olympia, WA

Now It's Time to Play Outside

Sung to: *Ten Little Indians*

C
Now it's time to play outside,

G₇
Now it's time to play outside,

C
Now it's time to play outside,

G₇   C
Where it's sunny and warm.

Additional verses: Now it's time to run and play; Now it's time to throw the ball; Now it's time to jump rope; etc.

Sue St. John
Oregon, OH

It's Time to Go Out And Play

Sung to: *The Bear Went Over the Mountain*

    C   F C
It's time to go out and play,

    G₇   C
It's time to go out and play,

                   F
It's time to go out and play,

    G₇   C
With all your friends today.

Judy Hall
Wytheville, VA

Outside Play

Sung to: *Twinkle, Twinkle, Little Star*

C   F   C
Let's go out to play today,

    G₇   C   G₇   C
The sun is shining, it's a beautiful day.

    G₇   C   G₇
We will hop and skip and run,

C   G₇   C   G₇
And we'll have a lot of fun.

C   F   C
Let's go out to play today,

    G₇   C   G₇   C
The sun is shining, it's a beautiful day.

Patricia Coyne
Mansfield, MA

Exercise Our Muscles

Sung to: *Ring Around the Rosie*

C
Run around the playground.

Exercise our muscles,
             G   C
Growing, growing up so strong.

Additional verses: Swing on the swings; Climb on the bars; Dig in the sandbox; Bounce, bounce the balls.

Susan Peters
Upland, CA

Let's Go to the Playground

Sung to: *Did You Ever See a Lassie?*

F
Let's go to the playground,
   C₇   F
The playground, the playground,

Let's go to the playground,
C₇   F
Where we will swing.
   C₇   F
We'll swing and swing,
   C₇   F
And swing and swing.

Let's go to the playground,
C₇   F
Where we will swing.

Substitute the names of other playground activities for the word *swing*.

Susan Miller
Kutztown, PA

Climbing Up the Slide

Sung to: *Eensy, Weensy Spider*

     F   C₇   F
My itsy bitsy feet are climbing up the slide,
                 C₇   F
Down comes my body in a long glide.
            C₇   F
Up go my feet again, inching to the top,
               C₇   F
Down I slide real quickly to a great big stop.

Judy Hall
Wytheville, VA

Out On the Playground
Sung to: *Up On the Housetop*

D
Playing on the playground is a treat,
G   D   A
Swinging and sliding can't be beat.
    D
The playground is where we like to play,
G D   A   D
It is fun each and every day.
G   D
Fun, fun, fun, we like to run,
A   D
Fun, fun, fun, 'til we are done.
               G
The playground is where we like to play,
D   A   D
It is fun each and every day.

Judy Hall
Wytheville, VA

Playground Fun
Sung to: *Take Me Out to the Ball Game*

C   G
Let's go out to the playground,
C   G
Let's go out to the swings.
A₇   D_m
Seesaws and sliding boards, climbers too,
             G
I like the jungle gym, how about you?
      C   G
For it's run, jump, slide at the playground,
 C   F
If you don't have fun, it's a shame.
    F   C
Oh, let's sing, play, have a good day
   F G C
At the playground.

Betty Silkunas
Lansdale, PA

Down By the Playground
Sung to: *Down By the Station*

C   G   C
Down by the playground, early in the morning,
                  G   C
See the little seesaws all in a row.

All the swings and monkey bars,
G   C
And the slides are waiting,
        G
Waiting for the children,
     C
Ready, set, go!

Judy Hall
Wytheville, VA

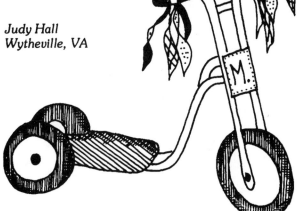

Swinging, Swinging
Sung to: *Sailing, Sailing*

C   F   C
Swinging, swinging on my special swing,
    G₇   C
When days are hot and days are cold,
D   G₇
Swinging on my swing.
C   F   C
Up high, down low, now reach for the sky,
   G₇   C
Oh, don't you wish that you were me
D   G   C
Swinging on my swing?

Susan Nydick
Philadelphia, PA

Playing All Morning

Sung to: *I've Been Working On the Railroad*

G
We've been playing on the playground
C   G
All the morning long.

We've been playing on the playground
D₇   G
Having fun and singing songs.

Barbara Robinson
Glendale, AR

I Am Swinging

Sung to: *Frere Jacques*

C
I am swinging, I am swinging,

Up so high, up so high.

First I swing forward,

Then I swing backward.

Touch the sky, touch the sky.

Susan Nydick
Philadelphia, PA

Playground Song

Sung to: *Mary Had a Little Lamb*

C
I like to climb on the jungle gym,
G₇   C
Jungle gym, jungle gym.

I like to climb on the jungle gym
G₇   C
On the big playground.

C
I like to go up in the swing,
G₇   C
In the swing, in the swing.

I like to go up in the swing
G₇   C
On the big playground.

C
I like to go down the steep slide,
G₇   C
The steep slide, the steep slide.

I like to go down the steep slide
G₇   C
On the big playground.

Barbara B. Fleisher
Glen Oaks, NY

Come With Me

Sung to: *Row, Row, Row Your Boat*

C
Come, come, come with me,

Time to go inside.

Line up straight and quietly,
G   C
Then please follow me.

Cindy Dingwall
Palatine, IL

Stand In Line

Sung to: *She'll Be Coming Round the Mountain*

            F
If you're wearing tennis shoes stand in line,
                                                        C
If you're wearing tennis shoes stand in line.
            F
If you're wearing tennis shoes,
            B♭
If you're wearing tennis shoes,
            F   C₇   F
If you're wearing tennis shoes stand in line.

Substitute other clothing names for the words *tennis shoes* until all of the children are in line.

Betty Silkunas
Lansdale, PA

Ready to Go Outside
Sung to: *When the Saints Go Marching In*

           C
Oh, when we all, oh, when we all,

                         G_7
Oh, when we all are standing still,

      C   F
We will be ready to go outside,

        C G_7 C
When we all are standing still.

Ellen Javernick
Loveland, CO

Move So Fine In Line
Sung to: *Hokey-Pokey*

C
We keep our eyes straight ahead,

We keep our hands at our side,

We keep our feet so, so quiet,

  G
As right out the door we glide.

We move so fine in line,

No one turns themselves around —

             C
That's what it's all about!

Betty Silkunas
Lansdale, PA

Line Up
Sung to: *Skip to My Lou*

F
Line up, line up, get in line,

C_7
Line up, line up, get in line,

F
Line up, line up, get in line,

C_7 F
We're going to go to lunch.

Substitute the name of your next activity for the
word *lunch*.

Sue Brown
Louisville, KY

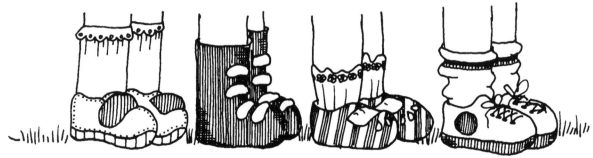

Happy Helpers

Sung to: *You Are My Sunshine*

Teacher:

        C
We need some helpers, some happy helpers

    F   C
To help us clean up the room today.

Children:

       F   C
We are your helpers, and we will help you

    G₇   C
Put all the toys away.

Florence Dieckmann
Roanoke, VA

All Day Long

Sung to: *Mary Had a Little Lamb*

C
Molly is in charge of blocks,

 G₇   C
In charge of blocks, in charge of blocks.

Molly is in charge of blocks,

G₇   C
All day long.

Substitute one of your children's names for the name *Molly*, and the appropriate job for the phrase *in charge of blocks*.

Ann-Marie Donovan
Framingham, MA

Need Our Helpers

Sung to: *Oh, My Darling Clementine*

F
Need our helpers, need our helpers,

            C₇
Need our helpers today,

                     F
Time for helpers to do their jobs,

        C₇   F
Need our helpers today.

F
Water plants, water plants,

                   C₇
Water plants so they grow strong,

              F
Time to water our nice plants,

       C₇   F
Need our helpers today.

F
Pass out papers, pass out papers,

                C₇
Pass out papers to our class,

                 F
Please help me pass out papers,

       C₇   F
Need our helpers today.

Create your own verses as needed.

Cindy Dingwall
Palatine, IL

I'm a Helper
Sung to: *London Bridge*

C
I'm a helper; yes, I am,
G   C
Yes, I am; yes, I am.

I'm a helper; yes, I am,
G   C
I'm a helper.

C
I will close the door today,
G   C
Door today, door today.

I will close the door today,
G   C
I'm a helper.

Additional verses: I will be the leader today; I will turn on the lights today; I will feed the fish today; I will mark the calendar today; etc.

Rita Galloway
Harlingen, TX

Good Helpers
Sung to: *The Farmer In the Dell*

      D
Good helpers we will be,

Good helpers we will be.

We pick up our toys and put them away
       A₇   D
Good helpers we will be.

Substitute the names of other items to be put away for the word *toys*.

Linda Ferguson
Olympia, WA

Today's Helpers
Sung to: *The Mulberry Bush*

C
Todd will be the helper today,
G
Helper today, helper today.
C
Todd will be the helper today,
G   C
He will put the blocks away.

Substitute the name of one of your children for the name *Todd,* and the appropriate job for the phrase *put the blocks away.*

Barbara Paxson
Warren, OH

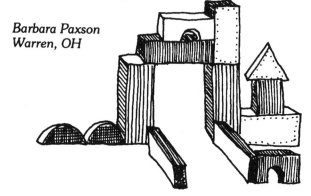

It's Time to Put Our Things Away

Sung to: *Twinkle, Twinkle, Little Star*

C   F   C
We've had lots of fun today,

    G₇   C   G₇   C
It's time to put our things away.

       G₇   C   G₇
We need all the girls and boys

C   G₇   C   G₇
To stop now and pick up toys.

C   F   C
We've had lots of fun today,

    G₇   C   G₇   C
It's time to put our things away.

*Ann-Marie Donovan
Framingham, MA*

Pick Up the Toys

Sung to: *Ten Little Indians*

C
Pick up the toys and put them away,

G₇
Pick up the toys and put them away,

C
Pick up the toys and put them away,

G₇   C
It is cleanup time.

Additional verses: Pick up the puzzles and put them together; Pick up the books and put them on the shelf; Pick up the blocks and put them in the box; Look at the room, it's neat and tidy; Thank you, thank you all for helping.

*Cindy Dingwall
Palatine, IL*

Time to Clean Up

Sung to: *Oh, My Darling Clementine*

       F
Time to clean up, time to clean up,

              C₇
Time to clean up right away.

                F
Time to clean up, time to clean up,

  C₇   F
'Cause now it's time to play.

Additional verses: Stack your crayons; Pick up your trash; Fix your papers; Pack up your things.

*Lois Putnam
Pilot Mt., NC*

Room Cleanup
Sung to: *The Farmer In the Dell*

      D
We're cleaning up our room,

The job will be done soon.

It's fun to put the toys away
     A₇   D
While we sing a happy tune.

Susan Burbridge
Beavercreek, OH

We're Picking Up Our Toys
Sung to: *The Farmer In the Dell*

     D
We're picking up our toys

We're picking up our toys,

Heigh-ho-the-derry-oh
     A₇   D
We're picking up our toys.

Additional verses: We're picking up our books; We're picking up our puzzles; We're picking up our games; etc.

Lois Olson
Webster City, IA

After We Play
Sung to: *Twinkle, Twinkle, Little Star*

C   F   C
After we play with the toys,
  G₇   C   G₇   C
We join the other girls and boys
      G₇   C   G₇
In helping put the things away
   C   G₇   C   G₇
So we can play another day.
C   F   C
We're proud of the job we've done,
  G₇   C   G₇ C
Because it was shared by everyone.

Susan Burbridge
Beavercreek, OH

Put Our Toys Away
Sung to: *Mary Had a Little Lamb*

C
Let's all put our toys away,

G₇   C
Toys away, toys away.

Let's all put our toys away,

      G₇   C
And sit down with our friends.

Bev Qualheim
Marquette, MI

Let's All Join In
Sung to: *If You're Happy And You Know It*

  G   D
It's cleanup time, let's all join in,

                      G
It's cleanup time, let's all join in.

  C
All the girls and all the boys,

    G
Let's put away the toys,

  D   G
It's cleanup time, let's all join in.

Kristina Carle and Nanette Belice
Kensington, MD

Put Them All Away
Sung to: *Skip to My Lou*

F
Pick your toys up off the floor,

C₇
Pick your toys up off the floor,

F
Pick your toys up off the floor.

      G   F
And put them all away.

Additional verses: Pick your games up off the table;
Pick your books up off the floor; etc.

Rita Galloway
Harlingen, TX

Let's All Work Together
Sung to: *Jingle Bells*

F
Cleanup time, cleanup time,

Let's put the toys away.
C₇   F
Let's all work together now
    G₇   C₇
To clean our room today.
F
Cleanup time, cleanup time,

Let's put the toys away.
C₇   F
Let's all work together now
    C₇   F
To clean our room today.

Rita Galloway
Harlingen, TX

Cleanup Time Today
Sung to: *Row, Row, Row Your Boat*

C
Clean, clean, it's time to clean,

Cleanup time today.

Books and blocks and all your toys,
G   C
Put them all away.

Carol Kyger
Hood River, OR

Let's Pick Up Today
Sung to: *The Mulberry Bush*

C
Let's pick up the blocks today,
       G
The blocks today, the blocks today.
C
Let's pick up the blocks today,
      G   C
And put them all away.

Additional verses: Let's pick up the toys today; Let's pick up the books today; Let's pick up the puzzles today; etc.

Susan Miller
Kutztown, PA

Everyone's a Helper

Sung to: *Frere Jacques*

C
Time for cleanup, time for cleanup

Everyone, everyone.

We all work together,

We all work together.

Cleanup time, cleanup time.

C
Pick up the toys, pick up the toys

Put them away, put them away.

Everyone's a helper,

Everyone's a helper.

Thank you Zak, thank you Anne.

Substitute the names of your children for the names *Zak* and *Anne*.

Linda Meisch
Lincoln Park, NJ

It's Time to Stop Now

Sung to: *London Bridge*

    C
It's time to stop now and clean up,
G   C
And clean up, and clean up.

It's time to stop now and clean up,
G   C
Then we'll have our snack.

Substitute the name of the next activity for the phrase *have our snack*.

Ann-Marie Donovan
Framingham, MA

Put Your Work Away

Sung to: *Twinkle, Twinkle, Little Star*

C   F   C
Stop and put your work away,
G₇ C   G₇   C
It is time to end the day.
         G₇   C   G₇
We have worked, and we have played
     C   G₇   C   G₇
We'll come again another day.
C   F   C
Stop and put your work away,
G₇ C   G₇   C
It is time to end the day.

Betty Ruth Baker
Waco, TX

It's Time to Clean Up
Sung to: *Mary Had a Little Lamb*

C
Do you know what time it is,
G₇   C
Time it is, time it is?

Do you know what time it is?
  G₇   C
It's time to clean up.

Betty Ruth Baker
Waco, TX

Cleanup Pokey
Sung to: *Hokey-Pokey*

C
You pick your first block up,

You put your first block down,

You pick your next block up,
          G
And you shake it all around.

You do the cleanup pokey,

And you put your things away —
                    C
That's what it's all about.

Judy Hall
Wytheville, VA

Cleanup Time
Sung to: *Happy Birthday*

      F   C   F
It's time to clean up, it's time to clean up,
              B♭   F   C F
It's time to clean up, put the toys away.

  F   C   F
I need Sean to help, I need Sean to help,
              B♭   F   C F
I need Sean to help me put this book away.

  F   C   F
I like what I see, I like what I see,
              B♭   F   C F
I like what I see, you clean up so well.

Substitute the name of one of your children for the
name *Sean,* and the name of an item to be put away
for the word *book.*

Renee Lowry
Canoga Park, CA

We'll Be Ready For Our Parents

Sung to: *She'll Be Coming Round the Mountain*

     F
We'll be ready for our parents when they come,

                                          C₇
We'll be ready for our parents when they come.

     F
We'll be sitting nice and quiet,

      B♭
Please get ready, won't you try it?

     F   C₇   F
We'll be ready for our parents when they come.

Cindy Dingwall
Palatine, IL

Good-Bye Song

Sung to: *Goodnight Ladies*

F   C
Good-bye Brian, good-bye Cindy,

F   B♭   F   C   F
Good-bye Andy, it's time to say good-bye.

Substitute the names of your children for the names in the song. Shake hands with each child as his or her name is sung. Repeat until each child's name has been sung.

Paula Laughtland
Edmonds, WA

We Had a Happy Day

Sung to: *The Farmer In the Dell*

     D
It's time to go home,

It's time to go home.

Wave good-bye to everyone,

   A₇   D
It's time to go home.

     D
We had a happy day,

We had a happy day.

Wave good-bye to everyone,

   A₇   D
We had a happy day.

     D
We'll see you again,

We'll see you again.

Wave good-bye to everyone,

   A₇   D
We'll see you again.

Betty Ruth Baker
Waco, TX

Say Good-Bye
Sung to: *Brahm's Lullaby*

C
Say good-bye, say good-bye,

G
To our friends for tonight.

Have a good night and sleep tight,

C
We hope to see you soon.

F   C
You're my friend, I like you,

G₇   C
And I'll see you soon.

F   C
I'll have things to tell you

G₇   C
When I see you again.

Cindy Dingwall
Palatine, IL

Wave Good-Bye
Sung to: *Mary Had a Little Lamb*

C
It is time to wave good-bye,

G₇   C
Wave good-bye, wave good-bye.

It is time to wave good-bye,

G₇   C
Good-bye to our friends.

C
Now it is time to go home,

G₇   C
To go home, to go home.

Now it is time to go home,

G₇   C
To go home from school.

C
We're glad we came to school today,

G₇   C
School today, school today.

We're glad we came to school today,

G₇   C
To learn and work and play.

Betty Ruth Baker
Waco, TX

Daily Good-Bye Song
Sung to: *Yankee Doodle*

C   G₇
Now it's time to say good-bye,

C   G₇
We've had a lot of fun.

C   F
Good-bye, good-bye, good-bye, good-bye,

G₇   C
Our time at school is done.

F
Now it's time to say good-bye,

C
We've had a lot of fun.

F
Good-bye, good-bye, good-bye, good-bye,

C   G₇   C
Our time at school is done.

Linda Ferguson
Olympia, WA

Learning About Ourselves And Others

Stop, Look And Listen

Sung to: *Skip to My Lou*

C
Stop, look. Stop, look and listen,
G₇
Stop, look. Stop, look and listen,
C
Stop, look. Stop, look and listen,
    G₇   C
Before you cross the street.

Lois Putnam
Pilot Mt., NC

When We Go to School

Sung to: *Mary Had a Little Lamb*

C
This is the way we watch the lights,
G₇   C
Watch the lights, watch the lights.

This is the way we watch the lights,
G₇   C
When we go to school.

    C
We stop and wait if it is red,
  G₇   C
If it is red, if it is red.

We stop and wait if it is red,
G₇   C
When we go to school.

    C
We wait until the light turns green,
   G₇   C
The light turns green, the light turns green.

We wait until the light turns green,
G₇   C
When we go to school.

    C
We look both ways before we cross,
  G₇   C
Before we cross, before we cross.

We look both ways before we cross,
G₇   C
When we go to school.

    C
We walk directly to our school,
G₇   C
To our school, to our school.

We walk directly to our school,
G₇   C
When we go to school.

Sue St. John
Oregon, OH

Colors Of Safety

Sung to: *Twinkle, Twinkle, Little Star*

C   F   C
Red means stop and green means go,
G₇   C   G₇   C
Yellow's caution, we all know.
             F   C   G₇
Stoplights tell cars what to do,
C   G₇   C   G₇
We'll pretend that we're cars too.
C   F   C
Red means stop and green means go,
G₇   C   G₇   C
Yellow's caution, we all know.

Becky Valenick
Rockford, IL

Buckle Up

Sung to: *Twinkle, Twinkle, Little Star*

C   F   C
When I get into the car,
 G₇   C   G₇   C
I buckle up for near or far.
            F   C   G₇
It holds me in my seat so tight
C   F   C   G₇
I feel so safe, I know it's right.
C   F   C
I use my seatbelt every day,
 G₇   C   G₇   C
So I'll be safe in every way.

Susan Burbridge
Beavercreek, OH

Stop, Drop And Roll

Sung to: *Oh, My Darling Clementine*

F
I'm on fire, I'm on fire!

                      C
But I know just what to do.

                 F
I will stop all of my running,

        C₇   F
Drop and roll's the thing to do.

Becky Valenick
Rockford, IL

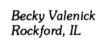

It's Important That I Know My Address

Sung to: *If You're Happy And You Know It*

F   C₇

It's important that I know my address,

It's important that I know my address.

Bᵇ

If you listen to me now,

F

I will say it, I know how.

C₇

It's important that I know my address.

Have each child say his or her address at the end of the song.

Cindy Dingwall
Palatine, IL

I Know My Phone Number

Sung to: *Twinkle, Twinkle, Little Star*

C   F C

I know my phone number, yes, I do.

G₇   C   G₇   C

Listen now, I'll say it for you.

    G₇ C

5-5-5 9-8-2-0,

C   G₇ C G₇

5-5-5 9-8-2-0.

 C   F C

I know my phone number, yes, I do.

G₇   C   G₇   C

Listen now, I'll say it for you.

Have each child substitute his or her phone number for the number in the song.

Cindy Dingwall
Palatine, IL

Seven Little Numbers

Sung to: *I'm a Little Teapot*

C   F C

Seven little numbers on my phone,

G₇   C   G₇   C

I learn them together to call my home.

                 F   C

Seven little numbers, what are they?

          F   G₇   C

My telephone number I learned today.

Have each child say his or her phone number at the end of the song.

Carla Cotter Skjong
Tyler, MN

Germs Will Make You Sick
Sung to: *Hokey-Pokey*

C
Germs are really mean,

But they can't be seen,

They will make you sick,
G
Then you will feel "ick."

Use some soap and water,

Scrub your hands to get them clean —
C
Clean's what it's all about!

Becky Valenick
Rockford, IL

Hand Washing Time
Sung to: *London Bridge*

C
Here we go to wash our hands,
G   C
Wash our hands, wash our hands.

Here we go to wash our hands,
G   C
Before we eat our snack.

Substitute other activities for the phrase
eat our snack.

Cathy Griffin
Plainsboro, NJ

Got My Toothpaste

Sung to: *Twinkle, Twinkle, Little Star*

C   F   C
Got my toothpaste, got my brush,

G₇   C   G₇   C
I won't hurry, I won't rush.

      G₇   C   G₇
Making sure my teeth are clean,

C   G₇   C G₇
Front and back and in between.

C   F   C
When I brush for quite a while,

G₇ C   G₇   C
I will have a happy smile.

Frank Dally
Ankeny, IA

Brush Your Hair

Sung to: *Jingle Bells*

F
Brush your hair, brush your hair,

Give your scalp a treat.

C₇   F
Part it, braid it, wear a hat,

    G₇   C₇
But always keep it neat.

F
Brush it once, brush it twice,

Keep it nice and clean.

C₇   F
Always comb the tangles out,

   C₇   F
And see the lovely sheen!

Lynn Beaird
Loma Linda, CA

Good Manners Is Thinking Of Others

Sung to: *My Bonnie Lies Over the Ocean*

C   F   C
Good manners is thinking of others,
            D₇   G
Good manners is doing what's right.
  C   F   C
Good manners is thinking of others,
    F   G   C
Good manners always feels right.
C   F
Helping, caring,
G   C
Sharing with you today, today.

         F
Kindness, honesty,
G   C
Sharing with you today.

Susan Peters
Upland, CA

Please And Thank You

Sung to: *The Muffin Man*

F
Please and thank you, how are you?
  G₇   C₇
Polite words will always do.
F
Friends feel good and you will too.
G₇ G   F
I can use them, how 'bout you?

Bev Qualheim
Marquette, MI

Manners Are the Way
Sung to: *The Farmer In the Dell*

F
Manners are the way,

To brighten up my day.

Please and thank you's what I say
  G   F
To brighten up my day.

Becky Valenick
Rockford, IL

Learning Manners
Sung to: *Camptown Races*

F
Learning manners can be fun,
C
Please and thank you,
 F
"Yes ma'am," "no sir" are some,
C   F
Say them every day.

When we learn them well,
Bb   F
You can always tell.

Pardon me, you're welcome too,
   C   F
Use manners every day.

Judy Hall
Wytheville, VA

Taking Turns

Sung to: *Mary Had a Little Lamb*

C
On the playground please take turns,
G₇   C
Please take turns, please take turns.

Remember others like a turn,
          G₇
And always try to share.

Patricia Coyne
Mansfield, MA

We Share

Sung to: *Twinkle, Twinkle, Little Star*

C   F   C
We share all our blocks and toys
G₇   C   G₇   C
With the other girls and boys.
              G₇   C   G₇
Crayons, scissors, paint and glue,
C   G₇   C   G₇
Puzzles, books, the easel too.
C   F   C
We take turns because it's fair,
G₇   C   G₇   C
And we're happy when we share.

Sue Brown
Louisville, KY

What I Do Best
Sung to: *Twinkle, Twinkle, Little Star*

C   F C
What thing can you do the best?
G₇ C G₇ C
Help us all so we can guess!
    G₇ C G₇
Can you lead or can you read?
C G₇ C G₇
Can you sing or pump a swing?
C   F C
Tell us, tell us, tell us, do,
G₇   C   G₇ C
Please, oh, please, give us a clue.

Janice Bodenstedt
Jackson, MI

Super Star
Sung to: *The Muffin Man*

  F
Oh, do you know a super star,
 G₇   C
A super star, a super star?
  F
Oh, yes, I know a super star.
  G₇ C F
The super star is me!

Paula Laughtland
Edmonds, WA

I'm Getting Better Every Day
Sung to: *Whistle While You Work*

  C
I'm learning how to count,

I'm learning how to count.
  G₇
I'm getting better every day,
     C
I'm learning how to count.

Additional verses: I'm learning how to write: I'm learning how to draw; I'm learning all the letters; I'm learning how to read; etc.

Ann-Marie Donovan
Framingham, MA

Who's Birthday?

Sung to: *The Muffin Man*

F
Oh, do you know the birthday boy,
G₇   C
The birthday boy, the birthday boy?
F
Oh, yes, I know the birthday boy,
G₇   C   F
The birthday boy is John.

F
Oh, do you know how old he is,
G₇   C
How old he is, how old he is?
F
Oh, yes, I know how old he is,
G₇   C   F
The birthday boy is four.

Substitute the name and the age of the birthday child for those in the song.

Paula Laughtland
Edmonds, WA

It's Your Day

Sung to: *Skip to My Lou*

F
Jason Smith, it's your day,
C₇
We're so glad you're five today.
F
Please stand up and show us how,
C₇   F
You turn around and take a bow.

Substitute the name and the age of the birthday child for those in the song.

Florence Dieckmann
Roanoke, VA

Birthday Fun

Sung to: *Row, Row, Row Your Boat*

C
Hurrah, hurrah, hurrah, it's grand,

Today is your birthday.

We hope you have a special time
G   C
With fun and games to play.

Bev Qualheim
Marquette, MI

A Reason to Celebrate

Sung to: *Twinkle, Twinkle, Little Star*

C   F C
Happy birthday, it's your day,

G₇   C   G₇ C
Hope it's great in every way.

    G₇   C G₇
We will help you celebrate

 C   G₇   C   G₇
'Cause we think you're really great.

C   F C
Happy birthday, it's your day,

G₇   C   G₇ C
Hope it's great in every way.

Rita Galloway
Harlingen, TX

Today Is a Special Day

Sung to: *London Bridge*

C
Today is a special day,

 G   C
A special day, a special day.

Today is a special day.

G   C
It's Wayne's birthday.

  (Place a birthday crown on child's head.)

C
Today Wayne is six years old,

G   C
Six years old, six years old.

Today Wayne is six years old.

G   C
It's Wayne's birthday!

Substitute the name and the age of the birthday child for those in the song.

Susan Miller
Kutztown, PA

Who Are We?

Sung to: *I've Been Working On the Railroad*

G
We've been working in the kitchen,

C   G
All the live long day.

We've been working in the kitchen,

       A₇   D
Making food along the way.

D₇   G
When you hear that it is lunchtime,

C   B₇
You'll know what we mean.

C   G
All the food that we've been making,

     D₇   G
Is the best you've ever seen.

(Who are we?)

We've been working in the office,

C   G
All the live long day.

We've been working in the office,

       A₇   D
Answering phones along the way.

D₇   G
When you're feeling kind of sickly,

C   B₇
You will come to us.

C   G
We will call your mommy,

     D₇   G
All without a fuss.

(Who are we?)

Judy Hall
Wytheville, VA

Thanks For All You Do

Sung to: *Yankee Doodle*

C   G₇
Thanks for all you do for us,
C   G₇
Mr. Green, you're special.
      C   F
You helped us with our work and play,
G₇   C
Thank you, Mr. Green.
F
You are special to us all,
   C
We needed you so much.
   F
We know you care and give your time,
     C   G₇ C
We love you, Mr. Green.

Substitute the name of one of your school helpers for the name *Mr. Green*.

Patricia Coyne
Mansfield, MA

Do You Know?

Sung to: *The Muffin Man*

F
Do you know the principal,
   G₇   C₇
The principal, the principal?
   F
Oh, do you know the principal?
   G₇   C₇   F
Her name is Mrs. Jones.

Substitute the title and name of one of your school helpers for the title *principal* and the name *Mrs. Jones*.

Judy Hall
Wytheville, VA

Concepts

Painting Fun

Sung to: *Twinkle, Twinkle, Little Star*

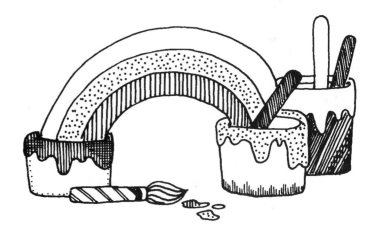

C   F   C
I know the colors for painting fun,
G₇   C   G₇   C
Green like grass and a yellow sun,
          G₇   C   G₇
An orange pumpkin and white snow,
  C   G₇   C   G₇
A red rose and a black crow,
C   F   C
Blue like a mailbox, brown like an ape,
 G₇   C   G₇   C
A pink pig and some purple grapes.

Ellen Bedford
Bridgeport, CT

Pretty Balloons

Sung to: *Twinkle, Twinkle, Little Star*

C   F   C
Pretty balloons in the air,
G₇   C   G₇   C
Lots of colors we see there.

       G₇   C   G₇
Red and yellow, green and blue
C   G₇   C   G₇
Can you see the colors too?
C   F   C
Pretty balloons in the air,
G₇   C   G₇   C
Lots of colors we see there.

Susan Burbridge
Beavercreek, OH

Rainbow Colors

Sung to: *Hush, Little Baby*

F   C₇
Rainbow purple, rainbow blue,
                   F
Rainbow green and yellow too.
              C₇
Rainbow orange, rainbow red,
             F
Rainbow smiling overhead.

F   C₇
Come and count the colors with me,
              F
How many colors can you see?
           C₇
One, two, three down to green,
             F
Four, five, six colors can be seen.

F   C₇
Rainbow purple, rainbow blue,
                   F
Rainbow green and yellow too.
              C₇
Rainbow orange, rainbow red,
              F
Rainbow smiling overhead.

Jean Warren

If You Are Wearing Red

Sung to: *If You're Happy And You Know It*

G   D
If you are wearing red, shake your head,

If you are wearing red, shake your head,
            G

C
If you are wearing red,

  G
Then please shake your head.

D   G
If you are wearing red, shake your head.

Additional verses: If you are wearing blue, touch your shoe; If you are wearing black, pat your back; If you are wearing green, bow like a queen; If you are wearing yellow, shake like Jell-O; If you are wearing brown, turn around; If you are wearing pink, give us a wink; etc.

Janice Bodenstedt
Jackson, MI

The Color Song

Sung to: *The Farmer In the Dell*

D
If you are wearing blue,

If you are wearing blue,

Stand up tall and turn around

A₇   D
And then sit right back down.

Repeat with other colors.

Ann-Marie Donovan
Framingham, MA

Yellow Balloons

Sung to: *Frere Jacques*

C
Yellow balloons, yellow balloons,

Floating up, floating up.

Never let them touch the ground,

Never let them touch the ground.

Keep them up, keep them up.

Have the children pretend to keep balloons up in the air as you sing the song. Sing the song as many times as desired, letting the children suggest other balloon colors.

Joyce Marshall
Whitby, Ontario

The Guessing Game

Sung to: *Mary Had a Little Lamb*

C
My friend has a green shirt on,
G₇   C
Green shirt on, green shirt on.

My friend has a green shirt on,
G₇   C
Can you name my friend?

Substitute the name of the color and the item of clothing one of the children is wearing for the words *green shirt*. Have the children try to guess which child it is.

Ann-Marie Donovan
Framingham, MA

Shapes In the Air

Sung to: *The Mulberry Bush*

C
This is a circle as you can see,

(Draw a circle in the air with your finger.)

G
You can see, you can see.

C
This is a circle as you can see,

G   C
Now draw it in the air with me.

Repeat for other shapes.

Neoma Kreuter
Ontario, CA

Holding Shapes

Sung to: *If You're Happy And You Know It*

        G   D
If you're holding a square, stand up,

                                    G
If you're holding a square, stand up.

        C
If there's a square in your hand,

        G
Then it's time for you to stand.

        D   G
If you're holding a square, stand up.

Repeat with additional verses about other shapes.

Judy Hall
Wytheville, VA

What Shape Is This?

Sung to: *The Muffin Man*

F
Do you know what shape this is,

        G_7 C
What shape this is, what shape this is?

F
Do you know what shape this is

        G_7 C   F
I'm holding in my hand?

Sing the song several times, holding up a different shape each time. Have the children name the shape at the end of the song.

Judy Hall
Wytheville, VA

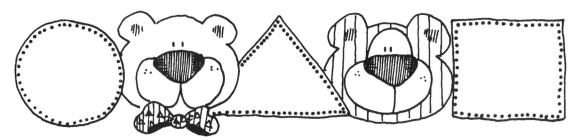

The Shapes Are On the Floor
Sung to: *The Farmer In the Dell*

D
The shapes are on the floor,

The shapes are on the floor.

Pick one up and guess its name,
A₇   D
And then we'll pick some more.

Place a variety of shapes on the floor. As you sing the song, have each child pick up a shape. At the end of the song, have each child name his or her shape then put it back on the floor.

Lindsay Hall
Wytheville, VA

The Square Song
Sung to: *You Are My Sunshine*

    C
I am a square, a lovely square,
        F   C
I have four sides, they're all the same.
      F   C
I have four corners, four lovely corners,
          G₇ C
I am a square, that is my name.

Rita Galloway
Harlingen, TX

Do You Know It's Name?
Sung to: *Mary Had a Little Lamb*

C
Do you know what shape this is,

   (Hold up a triangle.)
G₇   C
Shape this is, shape this is?

Do you know what shape this is?
G₇   C
Do you know its name?

C
Yes, I know what shape it is,
G₇   C
Shape it is, shape it is.

Yes, I know what shape it is,
G₇   C
It is a triangle.

Betty Ruth Baker
Waco, TX

The Triangle Song
Sung to: *Pop! Goes the Weasel*

D   A₇   D
I am a small triangle

            A₇   D
I have three sides you see.

    A₇   D
I also have three corners.

A₇   D
They're just right for me.

Rita Galloway
Harlingen, TX

Shapes
Sung to: *Frere Jacques*

C
This is a square, this is a square,

How can you tell? How can you tell?

It has four sides,

All the same size.

It's a square, it's a square.

C
This is a circle, this is a circle

How can you tell? How can you tell?

It goes round and round,

No end can be found.

It's a circle, it's a circle.

C
This is a triangle, this is a triangle

How can you tell? How can you tell?

It only has three sides,

That join to make three points.

It's a triangle, it's a triangle.

C
This is a rectangle, this is a rectangle

How can you tell? How can you tell?

It has two short sides,

And it has two long sides.

It's a rectangle, it's a rectangle.

Jeanne Petty
Camden, DE

When the Numbers March Right In

Sung to: *When the Saints Go Marching In*

         D
Oh, when the numbers march right in,

               A₇
Oh, when the numbers march right in.

D   G
We will count them one by one,

   D   A₇   D
When the numbers march right in.

        D
Oh, one-two-three and four-five-six,

            A₇
And seven-eight and nine and ten.

   D   G
When we finish all our numbers,

   D   A₇   D
We will count them once again.

Judy Hall
Wytheville, VA

Sing a Song Of Numbers

Sung to: *Sing a Song Of Sixpence*

C
Sing a song of numbers,

G₇
Count them one by one.

Sing a song of numbers,

    C
We've only just begun.

One-two-three-four-five-six,

F
Seven-eight-nine-ten.

G₇
When we finish counting them,

          C
We'll start them once again.

Judy Hall
Wytheville, VA

Counting Can Be So Much Fun

Sung to: *Row, Row, Row Your Boat*

C
One, two, three, four, five,

Six, seven, eight, nine, ten.

Counting can be so much fun
    G₇   C
Let's do it all again!

Substitute *Now it's time to end* for *Let's do it all again* the last time you sing the song.

Neoma Kreuter
Ontario, CA

Numbers

Sung to: *Oh, My Darling Clementine*

C
Count our numbers, count our numbers,
                    G₇
Count our numbers every day.
                C
It is fun to count our numbers,
    G₇   C
As a class every day.

C
One-two-three-four, five-six-seven-eight,
                G₇
Nine and ten we'll count today.
                    C
It is fun to count together,
    G₇   C
One to ten and then again.

Patricia Coyne
Mansfield, MA

Give It a Shakey-Shakey

Sung to: *Hokey-Pokey*

C
You put one finger up,

You put one finger down,

You put one finger up,
G
And you shake it all around.

You give it a shakey-shakey,

And you turn it all about —
C
That's how you learn to count.

C
You put two fingers up,

You put two fingers down,

You put two fingers up,
G
And you shake them all around.

You give them a shakey-shakey,

And you turn them all about —
C
That's how you learn to count.

Continue with as many verses as desired, up to ten.

Lois Putnam
Pilot Mt., NC

Show Me One

Sung to: *Skip to My Lou*

C
One, one, show me one,
G₇
One, one, show me one,
C
One, one, show me one.
G₇   C
Show me one right now.

Continue with as many verses as desired, up to ten.

Lois Putnam
Pilot Mt., NC

Alphabet Song
Sung to: *The ABC Song*

C   F   C
A is for apple, B is for ball,
G_7 C G_7 C
C is for candy, D is for doll.

C G_7 C G_7
E is for elephant, F is for frog,
C G_7 C G_7
G is for goose, H is for hog.

C   F   C
I is for Indian, J is for jam,
G_7 C G_7 C
K is for key, L is for lamb.

C   F   C
M is for monkey, N is for nail,
G_7 C G_7 F
O is for owl, P is for pail.

C G_7 C G_7
Q is for queen, R is for rose.
C G_7 C G_7
S is for scissors, T is for toes.

C   F   C
U is for umbrella, V is for vase,
G_7 C G_7 C
W is for wind blowing in my face.

C   F   C
X is for X-ray, Y is for you,
G_7 C G_7 C
Z is for zebra in the zoo.

Marie Wheeler
Tacoma, WA

Picking Up an A
Sung to: *The Paw Paw Patch*

F
Picking up an A and putting it in the basket,
C_7
Picking up an A and putting it in the basket,
F
Picking up an A and putting it in the basket,
C_7 F
Way down yonder in the letter patch.

Write alphabet letters on index cards and place the cards on the floor. Put a basket in the middle of the floor. As you sing the song, have the children pick up cards with the letter A written on them and put them in the basket. Continue with other letters as desired.

Judy Hall
Wytheville, VA

Where Has Our Letter Gone?

Sung to: *Where, Oh, Where Has My Little Dog Gone?*

C   G
Where, oh, where has our letter A gone?

G₇   C
Oh, where, oh, where can it be?

                        G₇
It is on a card that we had all along,

                      C
Won't you find it and show it to me?

Hide index cards with letters written on them around
the room. As you sing the song, have the children look
for the letter you name.

Judy Hall
Wytheville, VA

Found a Letter

Sung to: *Found a Peanut*

                 F
Found a letter, found a letter,

               C₇
Found a letter A today.

                   F
Oh, today I found a letter,

          C₇   F
Found a letter A today.

Substitute other letters as desired.

Judy Hall
Wytheville, VA

Calendar Song
Sung to: *The Mulberry Bush*

C
The calendar shows the name of the month,
G
The name of the month, the name of the month.
C
The calendar shows the name of the month,
G   C
For every month of the year.

C
The calendar shows the days of the week,
G
The days of the week, the days of the week.
C
The calendar shows the days of the week,
G   C
For every month of the year.

C
The calendar shows the dates of the month,
G
The dates of the month, the dates of the month.
C
The calendar shows the dates of the month,
G   C
For every month of the year.

C
Today is the first day of the month,
G
Day of the month, day of the month.
C
Today is the first day of the month,
G   C
Of the month of September.

Substitute the appropriate date and month for the words *first* and *September.*

Darlene Bursch
San Jose, CA

The Calendar
Sung to: *Twinkle, Twinkle, Little Star*

C   F   C
When we do the calendar,
G₇   C   G₇   C
We learn the month, the date and year.
G₇   C   G₇
Every weekday has a name,
C   G₇   C   G₇
There's lots of numbers that look the same.
C   F   C
So let's begin to show you how,
G₇   C   G₇   C
We do the calendar right now.

Susan Burbridge
Beavercreek, OH

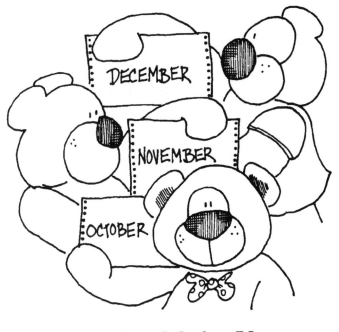

Months

Sung to: *Ten Little Indians*

C
January, February, March and April,

G₇
May and June and July and August,

C
September, October, November, December,

G₇　　　　　　　C
Now we've said them all.

Florence Dieckmann
Roanoke, VA

The Months Of the Year

Sung to: *Three Blind Mice*

C　　　G₇　　　C
January, February, March.

　　G₇　　C
April, May, June.

　　G₇　　　　C
July, August, September,

　　　G₇　　　　　C
October, November, December.

　　　　G₇　　　　　　C
These are the twelve months of the year.

　　　　G₇　　　　C
Now sing them together so we can all hear.

　　　　G₇　　　　C
How many months are there in a year?

　　G₇　　　C
Twelve months in a year.

Laura Copeland
Homewood, IL

There Are Seven Days

Sung to: *The Mulberry Bush*

C
There are seven days in the week,
G
Days in the week, days in the week.
C
There are seven days in the week,
     G   C
And now I'll say them all.

         C
There's Sunday, Monday and Tuesday,
G
Wednesday, Thursday and Friday.
C
Saturday ends our week, now,
G   C
Aren't you proud of me?

Patricia Coyne
Mansfield, MA

What Is Today?

Sung to: *The ABC Song*

C   F   C
Tuesday, Wednesday, Thursday, Friday
G_7 C G_7 C
Saturday, Sunday, today is Monday.

Start with the name of tomorrow's day. Point to each day on a calendar as you sing.

Cathy Griffin
Plainsboro, NJ

Every Week

Sung to: *London Bridge*

C
Every week has seven days,
G   C
Seven days, seven days.

Every week has seven days,
G   C
Can you name them?

C
Sunday, Monday, Tuesday, Wednesday,
G   C
Thursday, Friday, Saturday.

Sunday, Monday, Tuesday, Wednesday,
G   C
Thursday, Friday, Saturday.

Rita Galloway
Harlingen, TX

What Day Is It?

Sung to: *Mary Had a Little Lamb*

C
Do you know what day it is,
G_7 C
Day it is, day it is?

Do you know what day it is?
G_7 C
Today is Tuesday.

Substitute the appropriate day for the word *Tuesday*.

Betty Ruth Baker
Waco, TX

Yesterday, Today And Tomorrow

Sung to: *Frere Jacques*

C
Monday, Monday, Monday, Monday,

All day long, all day long.

Yesterday was Sunday,

Tomorrow will be Tuesday.

Oh, what fun; oh, what fun.

Substitute the names of the appropriate days for the words *Monday, Sunday* and *Tuesday*.

Linda Ferguson
Olympia, WA

Don't Forget the Day

Sung to: *You Are My Sunshine*

　　　　C
Today is Friday, it's really Friday,

　　　F　　　　　　　　C
From early morning, 'til late at night.

　　　　F　　　　　　　　C
While we are working, while we are playing,

　　　　　　　G₇　　C
Don't forget it's Friday today.

Substitute the name of the appropriate day for the word *Friday*.

Ellen Javernick
Loveland, CO

There Are Seven

Sung to: *Pop! Goes the Weasel*

D　　　　A　　　　D
Sunday, Monday, Tuesday, Wednesday,

　　　　　　　A　　　D
Thursday, Friday, Saturday.

　　　　　　A　　　　　D
Do you know what day it is?

A　　　　　D
Yes, it is Thursday.

D　　　　A　　　　D
Sunday, Monday, Tuesday, Wednesday,

　　　　　　　A　　　D
Thursday, Friday, Saturday.

　　　　　　A　　　　D
Do you know how many there are?

A　　　　　　D
Yes, there are seven.

Substitute the name of the appropriate day for the word *Thursday*.

Ann-Marie Donovan
Framingham, MA

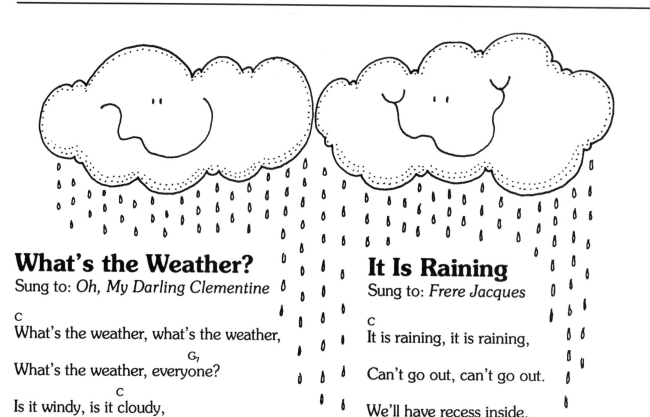

What's the Weather?

Sung to: *Oh, My Darling Clementine*

C
What's the weather, what's the weather,

               G₇
What's the weather, everyone?

         C
Is it windy, is it cloudy,

  G₇   C
Is there rain or is there sun?

Betty Silkunas
Lansdale, PA

It Is Raining

Sung to: *Frere Jacques*

C
It is raining, it is raining,

Can't go out, can't go out.

We'll have recess inside,

We'll have recess inside.

And have fun, and have fun.

Cindy Dingwall
Palatine, IL

Look Out the Window

Sung to: *Frere Jacques*

C
What's the weather, what's the weather,

On this Monday, on this Monday?

Let's look out the window,

Let's look out the window.

It is sunny, it is sunny.

Substitute the name of the appropriate day of the
week and the type of weather for the ones in the song.

Cindy Dingwall
Palatine, IL

The Wind Is Blowing

Sung to: *Mary Had a Little Lamb*

       C
The wind is blowing all around,

G₇   C
All around, all around.

The wind is blowing all around,

G₇   C
All around the town.

Judith McNitt
Adrian, MI

Mittens And Boots

Sung to: *Ride a Cock Horse*

C
These are our mittens,

F   C
What are they for?

     F   D
They keep our hands warm

        G   C
When we go out the door.

                F
And these are our boots,

        C   G
They will keep our feet dry

F   G
In piles of cold snow

       C   F C
When we play outside.

Bev Qualheim
Marquette, MI

Rain On My Umbrella

Sung to: *Frere Jacques*

C
Drip drip, drop drop,

Drip drip, drop drop,

Drip, drip, drop,

Drip, drip, drop.

Rain on my umbrella,

Rain on my umbrella,

Never stops.

Drip, drip, drop.

Betty Silkunas
Lansdale, PA

Bundling Up

Sung to: *The Mulberry Bush*

C
This is the way we put on our coats,

G
Put on our coats, put on our coats.

C
This is the way we put on our coats.

    G   C
To keep our bodies warm.

Additional verses: This is the way we put on our mittens to keep our hands warm; This is the way we put on our snow pants to keep our legs warm; This is the way we put on our boots to keep our feet warm; This is the way we put on our hats to keep our heads warm.

Janice Bodenstedt
Jackson, MI

In the Fall

Sung to: *She'll Be Coming Round the Mountain*

    F
Oh, the leaves turn brown and yellow in the fall,

                                       C_7
Oh, the leaves turn brown and yellow in the fall.

    F
Oh, the leaves turn brown and yellow,

    B^b
Yes, the leaves turn brown and yellow,

    F C_7 F
Oh, the leaves turn brown and yellow in the fall.

Betty Silkunas
Lansdale, PA

Frost Is In the Air

Sung to: *Sing a Song Of Sixpence*

C
Sing a song of winter,

G_7
Frost is in the air.

Sing a song of winter,

C
Snowflakes everywhere.

Sing a song of winter,

G
Hear the sleighbells chime.

Can you think of anything

    C
As nice as wintertime?

Judith McNitt
Adrian, MI

Sing a Song Of Springtime

Sung to: *Sing a Song Of Sixpence*

C
Sing a song of springtime,

G_7
Birds fill the air.

Plants are sprouting up again,

    C
And the weather's fair.

The sun is bright and warm with

G
Blossoms on the way.

Isn't it time for

    C
A wonderful spring day?

Elizabeth Vollrath
Stevens Pt., WI

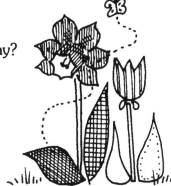

On the First Day Of Summer

Sung to: *The Twelve Days of Christmas*

     F   D_m   C   F
On the first day of summer, my true love gave to me,
         C   F
A robin in a maple tree.

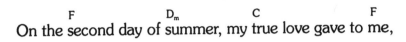

     F   D_m   C   F
On the second day of summer, my true love gave to me,

Two ducks a-waddling,
     F B♭ F   C   F
And a robin in a maple tree.

     F   D_m   C
On the third day of summer, my true love gave to me,

Three bees a-buzzing,

Two ducks a waddling,
     F B♭ F   C   F
And a robin in a maple tree.

       F   D_m   C
On the fourth day of summer, my true love gave to me

Four watermelons,

Three bees a-buzzing,

Two ducks a-waddling,
     F B♭ F   C   F
And a robin in a maple tree.

Additional verses: Five picnic baskets; six bright red apples;
seven ants-a-marching; eight swimmers swimming; nine
children playing; ten flowers blooming; eleven mowers
mowing; twelve gardens growing.

Suzanne Harrington and Wendy Spaide
North Wales, PA

Summer Fun

Sung to: *Frere Jacques*

C
It is summer, it is summer,

Lots of fun, lots of fun.

Swimming, picnics, playing,

Swimming, picnics, playing.

I'll have fun, I'll have fun.

Rose Lucio
Garden Grove, CA

Four Seasons

Sung to: *Twinkle, Twinkle, Little Star*

C   F   C
Flowers, swimming, pumpkins, snow,
G_7 C G_7 C
Make the seasons we all know.
      G_7 C G_7
Every year is the same,
C G_7 C G_7
And we give them each a name.
C   F   C
Summer, fall, winter and spring,
G_7 C G_7 C
Count the seasons as we sing.

Mrs. Bill Dean
Richland, WA

The Hands Are On the Clock

Sung to: *Hickory Dickory Dock*

C   G₇   C
Hickory dickory dock,

             G₇   C
The hands are on the clock.

                       F
One is long, the other's short —

C   G₇   C
Hickory dickory dock.

Judy Hall
Wytheville, VA

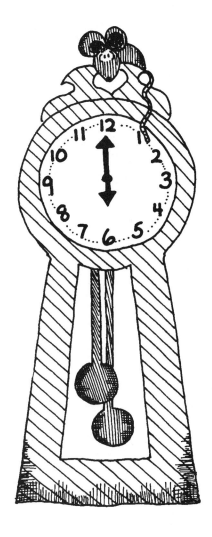

The Big Round Clock

Sung to: *The Wheels On the Bus*

     F
The big round clock goes tick tick tock,
C   F
Tick tick tock, tick tick tock.

The big round clock goes tick tick tock,
    C   F
To tell us the time.

     F
The hands on the clock go round and round,
C   F
Round and round, round and round.

The hands on the clock go round and round,
    C   F
To tell us the time.

Barbara Paxson
Warren, OH

Time

Sung to: *Ten Little Indians*

C
One o'clock, two o'clock, three o'clock hour,
G
Four o'clock, five o'clock, six o'clock hour,
C
Seven o'clock, eight o'clock, nine o'clock hour,
G₇   C
Ten, eleven and twelve.

Judy Hall
Wytheville, VA

What Time Is It?

Sung to: *The Muffin Man*

F
Do you know what time it is,
      G₇   C
What time it is, what time it is?
F
Do you know what time it is?
G₇   C   F
Let's look and see.

     F
It's 12 o'clock and all is well,
     G₇   C
It's 12 o'clock and all is well,
     F
It's 12 o'clock and all is well,
G₇   C   F
All is well today.

Substitute the name of the actual time for the words
12 o'clock.

Judy Hall
Wytheville, VA

Do You Know What Time It Is?

Sung to: *The Muffin Man*

F
Do you know what time it is,

G₇   C
What time it is, what time it is?

F
Do you know what time it is?

G₇   C   F
Look at the clock.

      F
The big hand is on the number 12,

      G₇   C
The number 12, the number 12.

      F
The big hand is on the number 12.

G₇   C   F
On our big clock.

      F
The small hand is on the number 2,

      G₇   C
The number 2, the number 2.

      F
The small hand is on the number 2,

G₇   C   F
On our big clock.

F
That means it is two o'clock,

G₇   C
Two o'clock, two o'clock.

F
That means it is two o'clock.

G₇   C   F
Time to go outside.

Substitute the names of the appropriate numbers,
time and activity for the ones in the song.

Cindy Dingwall
Palatine, IL

The Little Clock

Sung to: *I'm a Little Teapot*

C   F   C
I'm a little clock up on the wall,

G₇   C
Here is my big hand,

G₇   C
Here is my small.

If you listen carefully,

F   C
You will hear,

          F   G₇   C
Tick tock, tick tock, in your ear.

Judy Hall
Wytheville, VA

School Time

Sung to: *Frere Jacques*

C
What time's school time?

What time's school time?

On the clock, on the clock.

Show us when it's school time,

Show us when it's school time.

On the clock, on the clock.

Set out a play clock and have the children take turns showing you the time.

Additional verses: What time's snacktime? What time's lunchtime? What time's rest time? What time's playtime? etc.

Betty Silkunas
Lansdale, PA

A Clock's Face

Sung to: *Twinkle, Twinkle, Little Star*

C   F   C
My clock is like a great big face,
G₇   C   G₇   C
With hands moving from the nose place.
              G₇   C   G₇
The hour hand moves very slow,
        C   G   C   G₇
From 1 to 12 it must go.
        C   F   C
The hour hand won't say its o'clocks
        G₇   C   G₇ C
'Til the minute hand makes 60 tocks.

Ellen Bedford
Bridgeport, CT

TITLE INDEX

Totline®

Instant hands-on ideas for early childhood educators & parents!

This newsletter offers challenging and creative hands-on activities for ages 2 to 6. Each bimonthly issue includes • seasonal fun • learning games • open-ended art • music and movement • language activities • science fun • reproducible patterns and • reproducible parent-flyer pages. Every activity is designed to make maximum use of common, inexpensive materials.

Sample issue $2

*Individual and
Group Subscriptions Available*

Super Snack News

Sample issue $1

*Individual and
Reproducible
Subscriptions Available*

Nutritious food, facts and fun!

This monthly newsletter features four pages of healthy recipes, nutrition tips, and related songs and activities for young children. Also provided are portion guidelines for the CACFP government program. Sharing *Super Snack News* is a wonderful way to help promote quality childcare. A Reproducible Subscription allows you the right to make up to 200 copies.

TWO GREAT NEWSLETTERS

from the publisher of Totline books. Perfect for parents and teachers of young children. Get FRESH IDEAS. Keep up with what's new. Keep up with what's appropriate. Help your children feel good about themselves and their ability to learn, using the hands-on approach to active learning found in these two newsletters.

Warren Publishing House, Inc.
P.O. Box 2250, Dept. Z
Everett, WA 98203

TOTLINE® BOOKS

Hands-on, creative teaching ideas for parents and teachers

Activity Books

BEAR HUGS® SERIES
Remembering the Rules
Staying in Line
Circle Time
Transition Times
Time Out
Saying Goodbye
Meals and Snacks
Nap Time
Cleanup

BUSY BEES SERIES
Busy Bees–Fall
Busy Bees–Winter
Busy Bees–Spring

PIGGYBACK® SONGS SERIES
More books in this series!
Piggyback Songs
More Piggyback Songs
Piggyback Songs for
  Infants and Toddlers
Piggyback Songs in
  Praise of God
Piggyback Songs in
  Praise of Jesus
Holiday Piggyback Songs
Animal Piggyback Songs
Piggyback Songs
  for School
Piggyback Songs to Sign

1•2•3 SERIES
1•2•3 Art
1•2•3 Games
1•2•3 Colors
1•2•3 Puppets
1•2•3 Murals
1•2•3 Books
1•2•3 Reading & Writing
1•2•3 Rhymes, Stories
  & Songs
1•2•3 Math
1•2•3 Science
1•2•3 Shapes

MIX & MATCH PATTERNS
Animal Patterns
Everyday Patterns
Holiday Patterns
Nature Patterns

CUT & TELL SERIES
Scissor Stories for Fall
Scissor Stories for Winter
Scissor Stories for Spring

TEACHING TALE SERIES
Teeny-Tiny Folktales
Short-Short Stories
Mini-Mini Musicals

TAKE-HOME SERIES
Alphabet & Number
  Rhymes
Color, Shape & Season
  Rhymes
Object Rhymes
Animal Rhymes

THEME-A-SAURUS® SERIES
Theme-A-Saurus
Theme-A-Saurus II
Toddler Theme-A-Saurus
Alphabet Theme-A-Saurus
Nursery Rhyme
  Theme-A-Saurus
Storytime Theme-A-Saurus

EXPLORING SERIES
Exploring Sand
Exploring Water
Exploring Wood

CELEBRATION SERIES
Small World Celebrations
Special Day Celebrations
Yankee Doodle
  Birthday Celebrations
Great Big Holiday
  Celebrations

LEARNING & CARING ABOUT
Our World
Our Selves
Our Town

1001 SERIES
1001 Teaching Props
1001 Teaching Tips
1001 Rhymes

ABC SERIES
ABC Space
ABC Farm
ABC Zoo
ABC Circus

PLAY & LEARN SERIES
Play & Learn
  with Magnets
Play & Learn with
  Rubber Stamps
Play & Learn with Photos

SNACK SERIES
Super Snacks
Healthy Snacks
Teaching Snacks
Multicultural Snacks

OTHER
Celebrating Childhood
Home Activity Booklet
23 Hands-On Workshops
Cooperation Booklet

Cut & Tell Cutouts

NURSERY TALES
The Gingerbread Kid
Henny Penny
The Three Bears
The Three Billy
  Goats Gruff
Little Red Riding Hood
The Three Little Pigs
The Big, Big Carrot
The Country Mouse and
  the City Mouse
Elves and the Shoemaker
The Hare and the Tortoise
The Little Red Hen
Stone Soup

NUMBER RHYMES
Hickory, Dickory Dock
Humpty Dumpty
1, 2, Buckle My Shoe
Old Mother Hubbard
Rabbit, Rabbit,
  Carrot Eater
Twinkle, Twinkle
  Little Star

Story Books
with Activities

HUFF AND PUFF® SERIES
Huff and Puff's
  April Showers
Huff and Puff Around
  the World
Huff and Puff Go to School
Huff and Puff
  on Halloween
Huff and Puff
  on Thanksgiving
Huff and Puff's
  Foggy Christmas
Huff and Puff's Hat Relay
Huff and Puff's
  Hawaiian Rainbow
Huff and Puff Go to Camp

NATURE SERIES
The Bear and
  the Mountain
Ellie the Evergreen
The Wishing Fish

**Warren Publishing
House, Inc.**